PLAY and LEARN
Chinese

Ana Lomba *and* Marcela Summerville
with Lucy Lee

Illustrations by Pedro Pérez del Solar and Corne Cartoons/Enroc Illustrators

New York Chicago San Francisco Lisbon London Madrid Mexico City
Milan New Delhi San Juan Seoul Singapore Sydney Toronto

The McGraw-Hill Companies

This book is dedicated to Ana's beloved daughter, Marina,
a special-needs child who reminds us every day of the
miracle of learning.

1 2 3 4 5 6 7 8 9 10 11 12 13 14 15   CTP/CTP   1 9 8 7 6 5 4 3 2 1

ISBN   978-0-07-175970-0 (book and CD set)
MHID   0-07-175970-0 (book and CD set)

ISBN   978-0-07-175968-7 (book for set)
MHID   0-07-175968-9 (book for set)

e-ISBN   978-0-07-178169-5
e-MHID   0-07-178169-2

Library of Congress Control Number   2011929605

Interior artwork copyright © by Pedro Pérez del Solar and Corne Cartoons/Enroc Illustrators
Interior design by Think Design Group LLC

Acknowledgments

We would like to express our heartfelt thanks and appreciation to the many friends and colleagues who have encouraged and supported us along the way.
   A special thanks is due to the following people, who have facilitated book production and design:

- Pedro Pérez del Solar, illustrator, for his magical ability to bring our stories to life
- Corne Cartoons/Enroc Illustrators, for the wonderful new illustratons
- Bonnie Blader, Ana's dear friend and unofficial proofreader, for her golden touch with language, adding flair to the English translation
- Karen Young, our editor at McGraw-Hill, who guided us through the process of writing this book with keen insight and friendly advice

   We would also like to thank all those people in our personal lives who have made this book possible:

- Joseph, Victoria, Ana, Tyler, and Marina, our children, who are our constant inspiration
- Ozzie and John, our husbands, for their eternal patience—we couldn't have done it without you!
- Our readers and students, for being our best fans

McGraw-Hill books are available at special quantity discounts to use as premiums and sales promotions or for use in corporate training programs. To contact a representative, please e-mail us at bulksales@mcgraw-hill.com.

This book is printed on acid-free paper.

Contents

Introduction

Young children are to language what ducklings are to water. Let them jump in and play!

—Ana Lomba

Welcome to the brand new *Play and Learn Chinese*! It is because of forward-thinking and visionary parents, grandparents, and educators like you that tens of thousands of children are now using the *Play and Learn* series to learn Spanish, French, and now Chinese in early childhood—*the prime time for language learning*. Bravo! **hǎo jí le 好级了**!

How to Approach Chinese?

We gave a lot of thought to this question: What would a western parent need to tackle a complex language such as Mandarin Chinese in an immersive fashion that goes beyond memorizing a few colors, numbers, and animals?

The goal of this book is to help children develop basic everyday listening and speaking skills in Chinese. Fortunately for non-Chinese speakers, there is a phonetic device for pronouncing Chinese words called "Pinyin." Pinyin is an official transliteration of the Chinese characters based on the Latin alphabet and is taught in schools in China as a way to help children associate each character with its standard pronunciation. If you are wondering what Pinyin looks like, just take a look at the sentences appearing over the Chinese characters. These sentences are written in Pinyin.

You'll also see that this book uses simplified Chinese characters, the form of characters used in China today. Even though the goal of this book is to focus on speaking and listening communication skills, you can still practice writing the characters that accompany the vocabulary pictures. If your child wants to move on to the next level and begin to write Chinese, we recommend that you enroll your child in a formal course.

In order to help you and your child recognize and acquire some words from the very beginning, we decided to highlight a few words in each situation (they are marked in bold). We recommend that you focus on learning these words first. Though learning these words alone will not be enough to communicate in Chinese, using them will feel like progress to you and your child, and building momentum is one of the best things you can do at this point of language learning. As you continue listening to and using this book, you will be able to remember more words and even entire phrases and sentence structures.

Concerning the content, we decided to stick with situations familiar to western families. Otherwise, there would be a risk of not being able to use the new language very often, and that's what this book is all about—using the language in your everyday life. That being said, the "Do You Know?" sidebars provide useful information about Chinese culture and daily life.

Our goal with *Play and Learn Chinese* is to help users develop basic everyday listening and speaking skills. It would be beyond the scope of this book to target literacy skills. This book is meant as a starting point, and we highly recommend that you take classes (ideally with your child) to advance more rapidly in Chinese.

Helpful Tips for Pronouncing Mandarin Chinese

Chinese is a tonal language. Tones are marked over the Pinyin vowels as shown here:

- **First tone:** a flat high tone. For example mā 妈, which means mother.
- **Second tone:** a rising tone. For example má 麻, which means numb.

- **Third tone:** a tone that first falls and then rises. For example mǎ 马, which means horse.
- **Fourth tone:** a falling tone. For example mà 骂, which means to scold.
- **Neutral tone:** a light tone without any accent mark. For example ma 吗, which is a word used to mark a question.

Chinese consonants.
Most Chinese consonants are similar to English consonants except for the following list:

Mandarin Phonetics	English Equivalent Pronunciation
c	as the "ts" in "hats"
ch	as the "ch" in "church," with the tongue tip curled back
s	as the "s" in "sun"
sh	as the "sh" in "shirt," with the tongue tip curled back
z	as the "ds" in "reads"
zh	as the "j" in "just," with the tongue tip curled back
r	as the "r" in "ray," with the tongue tip curled back
j	as the "j" in "jeep"
q	as the "ch" in "cheat"
w	as the "w" in "wool"
x	as the "sh" in "sheet"
y	as the "y" in "yes"

Basic Chinese Vowels

Mandarin Phonetics	English Equivalent Pronunciation
a	as the "a" in "father"
e	as the "uh" sound in "bug"
i	as in "bee"
o	as the "o" in "oar"
u	as the "oo" in "too"
ü	like French u or German ü (say "ee" with rounded lips)

Ana Lomba's Easy Immersion® Method

There is plenty of research today showing that early childhood is the prime time for learning languages. We also know that young children learn languages best in interactive exchanges with their parents or teachers.

Unfortunately, over the last few years there has been a spike of flashcard-based foreign language programs especially targeted to young children. While your child may learn a few words and phrases from these programs, this type of approach is quite detrimental in the long run, as precious time is wasted on activities that do not lead to authentic real-life proficiency. Your child will learn much more in the meaningful context of playing and speaking with you!

Ana's breakthrough method ("Ana Lomba's Easy Immersion®") is based on three principles:
- Young children learn a new language best when they use it in everyday situations.
- Young children learn a new language best when they use it to interact with their parents, teachers, and friends.
- Young children learn a new language best when there is a bridge between home and school.

Many adults teaching Chinese or other languages to young children are not native speakers, nor do they hold degrees in language education (much less in early language education). This, however, should not be seen as an impediment to teaching the language. Moreover, it should not be seen as an impediment to teaching in an immersive way.

The fact that you are not fluent in Chinese or that you are a total beginner in Chinese does not mean that you can only teach words to your kids. It just means that you will need more support in order to teach the language. This is where Ana Lomba's Easy Immersion® comes to the rescue. Ana's materials provide content and how-to knowledge for non-native and native speaking parents and teachers who want to teach languages in a way that targets real-life proficiency.

Play and Learn Chinese and Ana's other materials are designed to assist parents and teachers who:

- Are serious about learning Chinese with their children
- Look forward to the challenges and the rewards of learning a new language
- Believe that they can be the initial motor that sparks their children's world language education

The word "easy" in Ana Lomba's Easy Immersion® does not mean that learning Chinese will always be easy. Instead, it is used to make a distinction between your experience in using Ana's method and the experience of landing in a foreign country where you do not speak a word of the language. As you will discover with *Play and Learn Chinese*, you will immediately understand the content and be able to use it with your children.

On a final note, when you start using this book and Ana Lomba's Easy Immersion®, you may think that the speakers on the accompanying audio talk too fast. This is to be expected! You are immersing yourself in naturally flowing speech after all. Give it time for the language to sink in and become your own. This is no different than listening to a song for the first time and trying to remember all the lyrics. Each time you will understand more, and soon enough you will be able to use the new language even in spontaneous conversation.

How to Use this Book

Start with the activities that are most interesting to your child. This program isn't based on a linear progression. Begin with an activity you think your child will enjoy and proceed as you wish. Some situations are easier and others more complicated; thus the activities and conversations accommodate different ages and language levels.

Use the illustrations as a picture dictionary. Visual input will help strengthen understanding, accelerate oral fluency, and facilitate emerging literacy in the new language. Read the captions at the bottom of the pages while pointing to the pictures and asking your child simple questions such as, *"Which word means fork in Chinese?" "What is this?"* or *"Can you say the names of these things?"* Whenever you are ready, try to ask these questions in Chinese.

Target words initially and move on to phrases as you go. Key Chinese words are **boldfaced** to facilitate learning and help build new vocabulary. Children's lines appear in *italics*, which let you know when the child should speak and will help you be able to match what they say with the English translation.

Take it easy. We recommend taking baby steps. Don't try to learn everything at once. Follow the pace of you and your child. Start with the expressions or vocabulary words that you think will be most appealing to your child and then build on these words and expressions by using them in other situations as well.

Use the new language frequently. Set your own goals and work at your own pace. Be aware that frequency beats length—it is better to use the language frequently for shorter periods of time than to use the language occasionally for longer periods of time. Please try to make these moments feel as natural and as playful as possible, and always follow your child's lead.

Don't let pronunciation stop you. Traditional language learning programs put too much emphasis on pronunciation, which has proven to be counterproductive again and again. Your pronunciation will improve as you go. That being said, Chinese is a tonal language, which is an additional challenge to speakers of non-tonal languages. For this reason, language classes are highly recommended as well.

Make it playful. Your attitude is important. Young children respond better to exciting and playful endeavors than to formal "sit-and-repeat" instruction. Make learning Chinese a fun activity.

Focus on your interaction with your child. The best way to learn a language is through personal interaction. Books, videos, and other materials will help, but they will never be enough. That is why we encourage you to speak to your child in Chinese. Never assume your child will effectively learn by simply parroting a DVD or video.

Don't be overly concerned about language "confusion." Mixing words, accents, and even grammatical structures is normal among young bilinguals. Contrary to common belief, this is not necessarily a sign of language confusion or of speech or language delay. Unfortunately, this common misunderstanding about early language learning is the cause of much unnecessary sacrifice for families who are advised to drop either the second language or the home language. If you are concerned about your bilingual child's language development, seek the help of a speech therapist who specializes in bilingual issues and educate yourself on the topic as well.

"Teach-Like-a-Pro" Strategies for Teachers

While the *Play and Learn* books were initially created for parents, many teachers are using them as well. We appreciate our colleagues' trust and support, and we offer these strategies as our way of saying, "thank you!" We hope you find them helpful!

• **Work on a theme, not on isolated activities.** For example, you could create a unit based on a theme of winter and health. Young children tend to get sick a few times during the winter season, and this provides a great opportunity to talk about germs, going to the doctor, washing hands, and many other topics related to winter and health. Select scenes from the book connected to the theme.

• **Extend the theme and integrate subjects.** If you talk about Chinese New Year one week, and then about pandas and other Chinese animals the next week, your students will have a very hard time learning Chinese. They may remember a word here and there, but that's all. Instead, extend the topic for a few weeks and integrate content from other subjects. For example, in a "Winter and Health" unit, they could learn numbers and practice taking their friends' temperature (math and science), draw a snowman (art), and learn the names and functions for some parts of the body (science).

• **Work on all four language skills, but focus on speaking.** Integrating listening, speaking, reading, and writing from the very beginning is the magic key to take you further sooner. For very young children, "reading" may mean that *you* read a story to them, or that they pretend to read a book they have memorized in Chinese. Writing may mean practicing small motor skills and scribbling, or using a Chinese writing brush to play with writing characters. Older students can listen to the situations in this book (without reading) and try to figure out what is happening. Note, however, that nothing will motivate your students more than being able to speak, so make a point of practicing speaking every day. In the beginning, you could just ask students to repeat after you. To encourage independent speaking, ask frequent questions, especially "wh" and "h" questions (when, why, where, who, which, and how). Do all of this in Chinese, of course!

• **Establish a school-home connection.** Recommend resources such as *Play and Learn Chinese* and Ana's other materials to your students' parents and encourage them to learn Chinese with their children. *No other formula is more powerful in early language education than the collaboration between teachers and parents.* That is why Ana's materials have been designed for use in school and at home.

We love hearing from families and teachers. If you use *Play and Learn Chinese*, let us know how you do!

zǎoshàng hǎo
早上好! — Good Morning!

gāi qǐchuáng lā
该起床啦!

Time to Get Up!

zǎoshàng hǎo gāi qǐchuáng lā
早上好! 该起床啦!

Good morning! It's time to get up!

xǐng yī xǐng xiǎo bǎobèi tàiyáng chūlái le
醒一醒、小宝贝、太阳出来了。

Wake up, honey. The sun is out.

gāi qǐchuáng lā zǎoshàng hǎo
该起床啦! 早上好!

It's time to get up! Good morning!

nǐ kàn tiānliàng lā **tàiyáng** chūlái le
你看、天亮啦。太阳出来了。

Look, it's daytime. The **sun** is out.

wǒ yào shuìjiào
我要睡觉!

I want to sleep!

wǒ zhīdào nǐ bùxiǎng qǐchuáng
我知道。你不想起床。

I know. You don't want to get up.

xiǎoxīn **lóutī**
小心楼梯。

Be careful with the **steps**.

mànmàn zǒu jiù zhèyàng zǒu
慢慢走、就这样走。

Slowly, that's it.

lái wǒmen dào **chúfáng** qù
来、我们到厨房去。

Come, let's go to the **kitchen**.

nǐ xiǎng chī shénme **zǎocān**
你想吃什么早餐?

What would you like for **breakfast**?

Did You Know?

Children in China usually eat rice porridge (zhōu 粥) with steamed buns (bāozi 包子, mántou 馒头) or soybean milk (dòujiāng 豆浆) for breakfast. They like to dip a fried breadstick (yóu tiáo 油条) in the soybean milk or rice porridge, similar to how bread is dipped in soup. Sometimes they eat pancakes (bǐng饼) and noodles (miàntiáo 面条) in the morning.

tàiyáng
太阳

wǒ yào shuìjiào
我要睡觉!

lóutī
楼梯

chúfáng
厨房

zǎocān shíjiān
早餐时间！

Time for Breakfast!

zǎocān shíjiān dào le 早餐时间到了。	It's time to have breakfast.
nǐ kě bù kěyǐ bǎ **wǎn** fàng zài zhuōzi 　shàng 你可不可以把碗放在桌子上？	Can you put the **bowls** on the table?
zhè shì **zǎocān gǔpiàn** hé **niúnǎi** 这是早餐谷片和牛奶。	Here is the **cereal** and the **milk**.
*wǒ xūyào **tiáogēng*** 我需要调羹。	*I need a **spoon**.*
nǐ yào bù yào **chéngzhī** *yào* 你要不要橙汁？要！	Do you want **orange juice**? *Yes!*
nǐ yào nǎ gè **bēizi lǜsè** de háishi 　**huáng sè** de 你要哪个杯子、绿色的还是黄色的？	Which **cup** do you want, the **green** one or the 　**yellow** one?
lǜ sè de 绿色的。	The green one.
zuò xiàlái chī zǎocān 坐下来吃早餐。	**Sit down** to eat breakfast.
Āiyō zāo le nǐ bǎ guǒzhī dǎfān le 哎哟、糟了！你把果汁打翻了！	Oh, no! You spilled the juice!
ná zhè gè zìjǐ cā gānjìng 拿这个、自己擦干净。	Here, clean yourself.

niúnǎi
牛奶

gǔpiàn de wǎn
谷片的碗

tiáogēng
调羹

bēizi
杯子

nǐ kànqǐlái zhēn piàoliàng/shuài
你看起来真漂亮 / 帅！

You Look So Beautiful/ Handsome!

yòng hěn gānjìng de **shuǐ**
用很干净的水、

*With very clean **water**,*

wǒ xǐ wǒde **liǎn**
我洗我的脸。

*my **face** I will wash.*

yòng yágāo hé **yáshuā**
用牙膏和牙刷、

*With toothpaste and a **toothbrush**,*

wǒ shuā wǒde **yáchǐ**
我刷我的牙齿。

*my **teeth** I will brush.*

bǎ **yágāo** fàng zài **yáshuā** shàng
把牙膏放在牙刷上。

Put the **toothpaste** on the **toothbrush**.

shuā shuā nǐde yáchǐ
刷刷你的牙齿。

Brush your teeth.

shuā shuā shuā shuā shuā shuā shuā
刷刷刷刷刷刷刷。

Chachachachachacha.

xiànzài yòng **shūzi**
现在用梳子、

*Now with the **comb**,*

wǒ shū wǒde **tóufa**
我梳我的头发。

*I will comb my **hair**.*

wǒ kàn **jìngzi** lǐ de zìjǐ
我看镜子里的自己。

*I look at myself in the **mirror**.*

wā wǒ kànqǐlái hěn piàoliàng/shuài
哇！我看起来很漂亮 / 帅！

Wow! I look so beautiful/handsome!

wā nǐ kànqǐlái zhēn piàoliàng/shuài
哇！你看起来真漂亮/帅！

Wow! How beautiful/handsome you look!

yágāo
牙膏

yáshuā
牙刷

shūzi
梳子

jìngzi
镜子

lái chuān yīfu
来穿衣服！

Time to Get Dressed!

wǒmen lái kàn kàn **yīguì** lǐ
我们来看看衣柜里。

Let's look in the **closet**.

kùzi qúnzi chènshān T xùshān
裤子、裙子、衬衫、T恤衫...

Pants, skirts, shirts, t-shirts . . .

nǐ xiǎng chuān shénme
你想穿什么？

What do you want to put on?

nǐ yào chuān **hóng sè** de qúnzi
你要穿红色的裙子吗？

Do you want the **red** skirt?

búyào yào zōng sè de duǎnkù
不要、要棕色的短裤。

*No, the **brown shorts**.*

bǎ **tuǐ** fàng jìnqù zài fàng lìng yī tiáo **tuǐ**
把腿放进去。再放另一条腿。

Put in your **leg**. Now your other **leg**.

lǜsè de háishi **huáng sè** de T xùshān
绿色的还是黄色的T恤衫？

The **green** t-shirt or the **yellow** one?

huáng sè de
黄色的。

The yellow one.

fēicháng hǎo bǎ nǐde **shoubì** fàng jìnqù
非常好。把你的手臂放进去。

Very good. Put in your **arm**.

zài fàng lìng yī zhī **shǒubì** nǐde **tóu**
再放另一只手臂。你的头...

Now your other **arm**. Your **head** . . .

dōu chuān hǎo le
都穿好了！

All done!

kùzi
裤子

qúnzi
裙子

chènshān/T xùshān
衬衫/T恤衫

duǎnkù
短裤

11

wǒmen dào wài biān qù
我们到外边去！ Let's Go Outside!

hěn lěng hěn rè
很冷！很热！

It's Cold! It's Hot!

jīntiān de **tiānqì** zěnmeyàng
今天的天气怎么样？

How is the **weather** today?

hěn lěng a
很冷啊！

It's so cold!

fēicháng lěng fēicháng lěng
非常冷！非常冷！

It's very cold! It's very cold!

wǒ chuān shàng **jiákè** yīnwèi fēicháng lěng
我穿上夹克，因为非常冷。

I put on my **jacket** because it's very cold.

wǒ dài shàng wǒde
我戴上我的 . . .

I put on my . . .

màozi shǒutào hé **wéijīn**
帽子、手套、和围巾

hat, gloves, **scarf**

yīnwèi fēicháng lěng
因为非常冷。

because it's very cold.

wǒmen jìnqù ba *à lǐbian hěnrè a*
我们进去吧。啊、里边很热啊！

Let's go inside now. *Oh, it's so hot inside!*

fēicháng rè fēicháng rè
非常热！非常热！

It's very hot! It's very hot!

wǒ tuō diào **shǒutào** yīnwèi fēicháng rè
我脱掉手套因为非常热。

I take off my **gloves** because it's very hot.

wǒ tuō diào wǒde
我脱掉我的 . . .

I take off my . . .

màozi **jiākè** wéijīn
帽子、夹克、围巾

hat, **jacket**, scarf

yīnwèi fēicháng rè
因为非常热。

because it's very hot.

màozi
帽子

jiákè
夹克

shǒutào
手套

wéijīn
围巾

lǎoshǔ hé xiézi
老鼠和鞋子

The Mouse and the Shoes

nǐde xiézi zài nǎli
你的鞋子在哪里？

Where are your shoes?

xiézi gēn lǎoshǔ zài yīqǐ
鞋子跟老鼠在一起。

*The shoes are with the **mouse**.*

lǎoshǔ tiào dào **zōng sè de xiézi** lǐ
老鼠跳到棕色的鞋子里。

A mouse went in a **brown shoe**.

xiézi zǒu tī tà tī tà xiǎng
鞋子走、踢踏、踢踏响。

The **shoe** went tap, tap.

lǎoshǔ tiào dào **lán sè de xiézi** lǐ
老鼠跳到蓝色的鞋子里。

A mouse went in a **blue shoe**.

xiézi zǒu tī tà, tī tà xiǎng
鞋子走、踢踏、踢踏响。

The shoe went tap, tap.

tiào dào **hēi sè de xiézi** lǐ
跳到黑色的鞋子里。

Went in a **black shoe**.

tiào dào **bái sè de xiézi** lǐ
跳到白色的鞋子里。

Went in a **white shoe**.

lái ba wǒmen yào zǒu le
来吧、我们要走了！

Come on, we have to go!

chuānshàng xiézi jì shàng nǐde **xiédài**
穿上鞋子。系上你的鞋带。

Put on your shoes. Tie your **shoelaces**.

kuài pǎo kuài pǎo lǎoshǔ lái le
快跑、快跑！老鼠来了！

Run, run! The mouse is coming!

zōng sè de xiézi
棕色的鞋子

lán sè de xiézi
蓝色的鞋子

hēi sè de xiézi
黑色的鞋子

bái sè de xiézi
白色的鞋子

wǒmen lái zuòcài
我们来做菜! Let's Cook!

wǒmen qù chāoshì
我们去超市

Let's Go to the Supermarket

nǐ yào zuò zài **tuīchē** shàng ma
你要坐在推车上吗?

Would you like to go in the **cart**?

zhè shì mǎi cài de dānzi
这是买菜的单子。

Here's the list.

wǒmen yào liǎng gè **qīngjiāo**
我们要两个青椒。

We need two **green peppers**.

yī gè liǎng gè liǎng gè qīngjiāo
一个、两个。两个青椒!

One and two. Two green peppers!

xièxiè bǎ qīngjiāo fàng zài tuīchē lǐ
谢谢。把青椒放在推车里。

Thanks. Put them in the cart.

wǒmen yào sān gè **yángcōng**
我们要三个洋葱。

We need three **onions**.

yī èr sān sān gè yángcōng
一、二、三。三个洋葱!

One, two, three. *Three onions!*

zhèr yě yǒu **dàsuàn**
这儿也有大蒜。

Here goes a head of **garlic** too.

yī lì dàsuàn
一粒大蒜。

A head of garlic.

hái yào shénme ā hái yào yī tiáo **miànbāo**
还要什么?啊、还要一条面包!

What else? Oh, the **bread**!

zhè tiáo miànbāo gěi nǐ
这条面包给你!

Here, a loaf of bread!

huángyóu suānnǎi hé **jīdàn**
黄油、酸奶和鸡蛋。

Butter, **yogurt**, and **eggs**.

dōu yǒu le wǒmen qù **fù qián**
都有了。我们去付钱。

That's all. Let's **pay**.

duōshǎo qián
多少钱?

How much is it?

qīngjiāo
青椒

yángcōng
洋葱

dàsuàn
大蒜

jīdàn
鸡蛋

14

yīqǐ lái zuòcài
一起来做菜！

Let's Cook Together!

nǐ néng bāng wǒ zuò cài ma
你能帮我做菜吗？

Will you help me cook?

shǒuxiān wǒmen yào xǐ **qīngjiāo**
首先我们要洗青椒。

First we need to wash the **peppers**.

ràng wǒ lái xǐ
让我来洗！

*I'll **wash** them!*

jiù xiàng zhèyàng qiē chéng xiǎo **kuài**
就像这样、切成小块。

Cut them in small **pieces**, like this.

xiànzài lái xǐ **xīhóngshì** hé **xīhúlu**
现在来洗西红柿和西葫芦。

Now let's wash the **tomatoes** and the **zucchini**.

qiē chéng xiǎo **fāng kuài**
切成小方块。

Now cut them in little **squares**.

zài **guōzǐ** lǐ fàng diǎn **yóu** xiànzài chǎo yī chǎo
在锅子里放点油。现在炒一炒。

Put **oil** in the **pan**. Let's fry them now.

Did You Know?

Children in China like to eat scallion pancakes (cōng yóu bǐng 葱油饼). This traditional appetizer is a pan-fried flatbread with minced scallions. Other ingredients, such as sesame seeds and green onions, are sometimes added. Another method of cooking scallion pancakes is to fry them with eggs coating one side. The pancakes are often served with soy sauce, hot chili sauce, or other dipping sauce. Red bean pancakes, eaten as a dessert, use sweet red bean paste instead of green onions and salt.

xīhóngshì
西红柿

xīhúlu
西葫芦

yóu
油

guōzi
锅子

wǔcān
午餐

	Lunch
wǔcān chī shénme 午餐吃什么？	*What's for lunch?*
tāng hé **yú** 汤和鱼。	**Soup** and **fish**.
zhèxiē chéng sè de dōngxi shì shénme 这些橙色的东西是什么？	*What's this orange stuff?*
shì **húluóbo** 是胡萝卜。	They're **carrots**.
wǒ bù xǐhuān húluóbo 我不喜欢胡萝卜。	*I don't like carrots.*
zhèxiē lǜ sè hé zōng sè de dōngxi shì shénme 这些绿色和棕色的东西是什么？	*And what's this green and brown stuff?*
shì **wāndòu** hé **ròu** 是豌豆和肉。	They're **peas** and **meat**.
wǒ bú è 我不饿。	*I'm not hungry.*
yě yǒu **bīngqílín** 也有冰淇淋。	There's also **ice cream**.
wǒ yào bīngqílín wǒ hěn xǐhuān nàgè 我要冰淇淋！我很喜欢那个！	*I want ice cream! That I like!*

Did You Know?

Chinese food is often prepared and served in small bite-size pieces, which makes it easy to eat with chopsticks. Chopsticks, called kuàizi 筷子, can also be used in the kitchen to beat eggs or stir and break up noodles. It is believed that chopsticks originated in China during the Shang Dynasty more than three thousand years ago. The use of chopsticks eventually spread out to other Asian countries.

húluóbo
胡萝卜

wāndòu
豌豆

ròu
肉

bīngqílín
冰淇淋

fēngkuáng tāng
疯狂汤

Crazy Soup

lái wǒ jiā kàn kàn
来我家看看
wǒmen hē de fēngkuáng **tāng**
我们喝的疯狂汤。
māma shuō
妈妈说、
zhuōbù wǎn tāng pánzi sháozi kāi
fàn lā
"桌布、碗、汤、盘子、勺子 – 开饭啦！"
bàba bǎ wǎn dài zài tóu shàng
爸爸把碗戴在头上。
jiějiě yòng chāzi qiē miànbāo
姐姐用叉子切面包。
gēgē yòng sháozi chī miànbāo
哥哥用勺子吃面包。
xiǎogǒu yòng dāozi hē tāng
小狗用刀子喝汤。
ài ài nǐmen duōme fēngkuáng
哎唉！你们多么疯狂！
wǒ yòng tāngchí hē tāng
我用汤匙喝汤。
èn wèidào zhēn hǎo
嗯！味道真好！

Come to my house and see

the crazy **soup** we eat.

My mom cries,

"**Tablecloth**, **bowls**, **soup**, **plates**, **ladle**–
Time to eat!"

*My **dad** wears his bowl on his head.*

*My **big sister** cuts the bread with a fork.*

*My **big brother** eats the bread with his ladle.*

*My **dog** eats his soup with a knife.*

Ay, ay! How crazy you are!

I eat soup with a spoon.

Ah! How tasty it is!

zhuōbù
桌布

wǎn
碗

pánzi
盘子

sháozi
勺子

bàn jiājiā
扮家家

Playing Kitchen

nǐ yào yòng wánjù **chúfáng** bàn jiājiā ma
你要用玩具厨房扮家家吗？

Do you want to play with the toy **kitchen**?

yào wǒ dāng **māma**
要、我当妈妈。

Yes, I'll be the **mom**.

hǎoba nàme wǒ dāng **nǚer**
好吧、那么我当女儿。

Okay, then I'll be the **daughter**.

wǎncān wǒ zhǔnbèi bāo jiǎozǐ
晚餐我准备包饺子。

I am going to make dumplings for dinner.

wǒ bǎ **guōzǐ** *fàng zài* **lúzǐ** *shàng*
我把锅子放在炉子上。

I put the **pot** *on the* **stove**.

māma **wǒ è le**
妈妈、我饿了！

Mommy, **I'm hungry**!

nǐ kěyǐ chī **bǐnggān** *zhǐ néng chī yī kuài*
你可以吃饼干、只能吃一块！

You can have a **cracker**, *but only one!*

qǐng nǐ bǎ **miànbāo lán** *fàng zài zhuōzi*
    shàng
请你把面包篮放在桌子上。

Please, put the **breadbasket** *on the table.*

yě yào fàng **bēizi**
也要放杯子。

The **cups** *too.*

wǒ kěyǐ yòng zhègè **jiǔbēi** ma
我可以用这个酒杯吗？

Can I use this **wine glass**?

nǐ shì **xiǎoháizi** *bù néng yòng děng nǐ*
    zhǎngdà ba
你是小孩子！不能用！等你长大吧。

You are a **kid**! *No way! When you grow up.*

māma wǎn fàn zhǔnbèi hǎo le ma
妈妈、晚饭准备好了吗？

Mommy, is dinner ready?

hǎo le xiān xǐ shǒu ránhòu kāi fàn
好了。先洗手然后开饭！

Yes. Wash your hands and lets eat!

guōzi
锅子

jiǔbēi
酒杯

miànbāo lán
面包篮

bǐnggān
饼干

wǎncān
晚餐

Dinner

wǎncān zhǔnbèi hǎo le
晚餐准备好了！

Dinner is ready!

wǒmen zuò xià lái chīfàn
我们坐下来吃饭。

Let's sit down and eat.

yǒu **kǎoròu**
有烤肉

There is **roast meat**

gēn **tǔdòu ní** hé **shālā**
跟土豆泥和沙拉。

with **mashed potatoes** and **salad**.

wǒ kě le
我渴了。

I'm thirsty.

zhè shì yī bēi **niúnǎi**
这是一杯牛奶。

Here's a glass of **milk**.

ná yī zhāng **cānjīn** zhǐ
拿一张餐巾纸。

Take a **napkin**.

yǒu shénme tián diǎn
有什么甜点？

What's for dessert?

yǒu **jiā nǎiyóu de cǎoméi**
有加奶油的草莓、

Strawberries with cream,

kěshì nǐ yào xiān chī wán **wǎncān** cái
    néng chī
可是你要先吃完晚餐才能吃。

but eat your **dinner** first.

kǎoròu
烤肉

tǔdòu ní
土豆泥

shālā
沙拉

jiā nǎiyóu de cǎoméi
加奶油的草莓

tián diǎn
甜点

Dessert

nǐ yào shénme tián diǎn
你要什么甜点？

What do you want for dessert?

wǒmen yǒu **júzi lí pútáo** hé
xiāngjiāo
我们有橘子、梨、葡萄和香蕉。

We have **tangerines**, **pears**, **grapes**, and **bananas**.

nǐ yào búyào yī gè júzi
你要不要一个橘子？

Would you like a tangerine?

yào yī gè júzi
要、一个橘子。

Yes, a tangerine.

wǒmen bǎ tā bō kāi ba
我们把它剥开吧。

Let's peel it.

yòng nǐde **zhǐjia** chuō jìnqù
用你的指甲戳进去。

Stick your **nail** in.

jiù xiàng zhèyàng nǐ kàn wǒ zěnme zuò
就像这样。你看我怎么做。

Like this. Look how I do it.

xiànzài xiàng zhèyàng bǎ **pí** lā kāi
现在、像这样把皮拉开。

Now, pull back the **skin** like this.

bǎ **yī piàn piàn** fēnkāi
把一片片分开。

Separate the **slices**.

yǒu hěn duō zhī
有很多汁！

It's so juicy!

Did You Know?

Most people in China eat fruit for dessert after a meal. Fruit selection changes with the seasons. People may also have a cup of tea during and after the meal. Drinking tea is an important part of Chinese people's daily life. Tea (chá 茶) is regarded as one of the seven daily necessities, the others being firewood (chái 柴), rice (mǐ 米), oil (yóu 油), salt (yán 盐), soy sauce (jiàng 酱), and vinegar (cù 醋).

júzi
橘子

lí
梨

pútáo
葡萄

xiāngjiāo
香蕉

wǒmen lái qīnglǐ chúfáng

我们来清理厨房

Let's Clean the Kitchen

*wǒ bǎ pánzi fàng jìn **xǐwǎnjǐ***
我把盘子放进洗碗机。

*I'll put the plates in the **dishwasher**.*

hǎo de bǎ **pánzi** fàng zài xiàbiān
好的。把盘子放在下边。

Okay. The **plates** go down here.

bǎ **bēizi** fàng zài shàngbiān
把杯子放在上边。

The **cups** go up here.

bǎ **dāochā** fàng zài lánzǐ lǐ
把刀叉放在篮子里。

The **knives and forks** go in the basket.

dìbǎn tài zāng le
地板太脏了！

*The **floor** is so dirty!*

wǒ yòng **sàobǎ** sǎodì
我用扫把扫地。

I'll sweep the floor with the **broom**.

zhè shì **lājī bòjī**
这是垃圾簸箕。

Here's the **dustpan** for the **trash**.

*dìbǎn háishi hěn **zāng***
地板还是很脏。

*It's still **dirty**.*

wǒmen **tuō** dìbǎn
我们要拖地板。

We'll have to **mop** the floor.

xiànzài chúfáng hěn gānjìng le
现在厨房很干净了！

The kitchen looks very clean now!

xǐwǎnjī
洗碗机

sàobǎ
扫把

lājī bòjī
垃圾簸箕

tuōbǎ
拖把

xiǎo yāzi tiào jìn shuǐ
小鸭子、跳进水！

Duckling, to the Water!

yùgāng zhuāng mǎn le wēnnuǎn de shuǐ
浴缸装满了温暖的水。

The **bathtub** is filled with warm water.

ràng wǒ bāng nǐ tuō diào nǐde **yīfu**
让我帮你脱掉你的衣服。

Let me help you take off your **clothes**.

xiǎo **yāzi** tiào jìn shuǐ guā guā
小鸭子、跳进水！呱, 呱。

Duckling, to the water! Quack, quack.

hēi búyào bǎ wǒ nòng shī le
嗨、不要把我弄湿了！

Hey, don't get me wet!

bì shàng nǐde **yǎnjing**
闭上你的眼睛。

Close your **eyes**.

wǒ yào bǎ shuǐ pō zài nǐde **tóufa** shàng
我要把水泼在你的头发上。

I'm going to pour water over your **hair**.

fàng yīdiǎn **xǐfàshuǐ**
放一点洗发水。

A little bit of **shampoo**.

wǒ yòng shénme lái xǐ xiǎo yāzi ne
我用什么来洗小鸭子呢？

What do I wash my duckling with?

zhè shì **hǎimián** hé **féizào**
这是海绵和肥皂。

Here is the **sponge** and the **soap**.

wǒ xǐ nǐde **shǒu**
我洗你的手。

I wash your **hands**.

wǒ xǐ nǐde xiǎo **liǎn** hé nǐ kěài de **bízi**
我洗你的小脸和你可爱的鼻子。

I wash your little **face** and your cute **nose**.

wǒ yòng shénme **cāgān** wǒde xiǎo yāzi ne
我用什么擦干小鸭子呢？

What do I **dry** my duckling with?

yòng zhè tiáo róuruǎn de **máojīn**
用这条柔软的毛巾！

With this soft **towel**!

yùgāng
浴缸

yāzi
鸭子

xǐfàshuǐ
洗发水

hǎimián
海绵

máojīn hǎimián hé féizào

毛巾、海绵、和肥皂

Towel, Sponge, and Soap

wǒmen lā kāi **yùlián**
我们拉开浴帘 . . .

We open the **shower curtain** . . .

wǒmen dǎkāi **shuǐlóngtóu**
我们打开水龙头 . . .

We turn on the **faucet** . . .

jìn qù shuǐ lǐ ba xiǎo bǎobèi
进去水里吧、小宝贝！

Into the water, honey!

*xiàng zhèyàng wǒ **xǐ** wǒde **tóufa***
像这样我洗我的头发。

*Like this **I wash** my **hair**.*

*xiàng zhèyàng wǒ xǐ wǒde **shǒu***
像这样我洗我的手。

*Like this I wash my **hands**.*

*xiàng zhèyàng wǒ xǐ wǒde **liǎn***
像这样我洗我的脸。

*Like this I wash my **face**.*

*xiàng zhèyàng wǒ **pō shuǐ***
像这样我泼水。

*Like this I **splash** water.*

*ó wǒ nòng le yī gè xiǎo **shuǐkēng***
哦！我弄了一个小水坑。

*Oh! I made a little **puddle**.*

cóng shuǐ lǐ chūlái ba xiǎo bǎobèi
从水里出来吧、小宝贝。

Get out of the water, honey.

lái ba, yòng zhè tiáo **máojīn** cāgān zìjǐ
来吧、用这条毛巾擦干自己。

Come and dry yourself with this **towel**.

féizào
肥皂

yùlián
浴帘

shuǐlóngtóu
水龙头

máojīn
毛巾

wǎnān
晚安!　Good Night!

wǒmen qù shuìjiào
我们去睡觉

Let's Go to Bed

wǒmen qù nǐde **wòshì**
我们去你的卧室。

Let's go to your **bedroom**.

zài zhèlǐ huàn tiáo **nèikù**
在这里、换条内裤。

Here, put on these **underpants**.

*wǒ yào chuān yǒu kǎchē de **shuìyī***
我要穿有卡车的睡衣。

*I want the **pajamas** with the trucks.*

hěn hǎo xiān bǎ **tóu** tào guò qù ránhòu bǎ
　　gēbo chuān guò lái
很好。先把头套过去、然后把胳膊伸出来。

Very well. First your **head**, then your **arms**.

xiànzài chuān **kùzi**
现在穿裤子。

Now the **pants**.

Yào bú yào qù **xiǎobiàn** búyào ma
要不要去小便? 不要吗?

Do you need to go **pee pee**? No?

qù cèsuǒ xiǎobiàn ba
去厕所小便吧。

Go to the bathroom and go pee pee then.

xiànzài qù shàng **chuáng** shuìjiào wǒ gěi
　　nǐ gài bèizi
现在去上床睡觉。我给你盖被子。

Get in **bed** now. I'll cover you.

*wǒ yào kàn nà gè yuèliang de **gùshi***
我要看那个月亮的故事。

*I want to read the **story** of the moon.*

hěn jiǔ yǐqián yǒu gè **yuèliang** zài tiān
　　shàng wēixiào
"很久以前有个月亮在天上微笑..."

"Once upon a time there was a **moon**
　　that was smiling in the sky . . ."

gùshi jiǎng wánle **qīn qīn** wǒ wǎnān
故事讲完了! 亲亲我晚安。

The end! Give me a goodnight **kiss**.

wòshì
卧室

shuìyī
睡衣

nèikù
内裤

chuáng
床

shuìjiào ba
睡觉吧

Go to Sleep

shuìjiào ba wǒde bǎobèi
睡觉吧、我的宝贝。

xiǎo **mìfēng** yǐjīng xiūxi
小蜜蜂已经休息。

xiǎo **niǎo** ér yě yǐ huí cháo
小鸟儿也已回巢。

huāyuán lǐ duōme ān wēn
花园里多么安温。

yuèliang zài **tiān** shàng wēixiào
月亮在天上微笑、

yī piàn yín guāng duō **měilì**
一片银光多美丽。

tòuguò **chuānghù** zhào zhe nǐ
透过窗户照着你。

shuìjiào ba wǒde bǎobèi
睡觉吧、我的宝贝。

kuài shuì kuài shuì
快睡、快睡！

Go to **sleep**, my sweetheart.

Little **bees** have been resting.

Small **birds** have returned to the nest.

The **garden** is quiet and warm.

The **moon** is smiling in the **sky**,

with its **beautiful** silver-colored light.

Through the **window,** the moonlight is shining
   upon you.
Sleep, my sweetheart.

Fast asleep, fast asleep!

yuèliàng
月亮

tiān
天

xīngxīng
星星

tàiyáng
太阳

yóuxì shíjiān
游戏时间！ Playtime!

zhuō mícáng
捉迷藏

Hide-and-Seek

wǒmen lái wán **zhuō mícáng**
我们来玩捉迷藏。

Let's play **hide-and-seek**.

wǒ bǎ nǐ de **xiǎogǒu** cáng qǐlai
我把你的小狗藏起来。

I'm going to hide your **doggy**.

bì shàng nǐde **yǎnjīng** shǔ shù
闭上你的眼睛数数。

You close your **eyes** and count.

yī èr sān sì wǔ
一、二、三、四、五 . . .

One, two, three, four, five . . .

wǒmen lái zhǎo xiǎogǒu
我们来找小狗。

Let's look for the doggy.

xiǎogǒu, nǐ zài nǎli
小狗、你在哪里？

Doggy, where are you?

wāng wāng wāng wǒ tīng dào xiǎogǒu jiào
"汪、汪、汪。" 我听到小狗叫！

"Bow wow, bow wow." I hear him!

zài bú zài **chuānglián** hòumiàn
在不在窗帘后面？

Could he be behind the **curtain**?

bú zài, tā bú zài zhèlǐ
不在、他不在这里。

No, he's not here.

tā zài bú zài **zhuōzi** xiàmiàn *bú zài*
他在不在桌子下面？ 不在！

Could he be under the **table**? *Nope!*

kěnéng zài **shāfā** hòumiàn *búzài zhèlǐ*
可能在沙发后面？ 不在这里！

Maybe he's behind the **sofa**? *Not here!*

wǒ zhīdào tā shì bú shì zài **chōutì** lǐmiàn
我知道。他是不是在抽屉里面？

I know. Will he be inside the **drawer**?

shì de tā zài zhèlǐ xiǎogǒu nǐ hǎo
是的、他在这里！ 小狗、你好！

Yes, he is here! Hello, doggy!

chuānglián
窗帘

zhuōzi
桌子

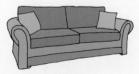
shāfā
沙发

chōutì
抽屉

wǒmen bǎ wánjù fàng hǎo
我们把玩具放好

Let's Put Your Toys Away

āi yā **fángjiān** tài **luàn** le
哎呀！房间太乱了！

Yikes! This **room** is a **mess**!

wǒmen bǎ **wánjù** fàng hǎo
我们把玩具放好。

Let's put your **toys** away.

bǎ **wáwa** fàng zài chuáng shàng
把娃娃放在床上。

Please put the **dolls** on the bed.

xiǎo **shìbīng** yīnggāi fàng zài nǎr ne
小士兵应该放在哪儿呢？

Where should we put the **soldiers**?

*fàng zài **xiāngzi** lǐ māma wǒ lái bāng nǐ máng*
放在箱子里、妈妈。我来帮你忙。

*In this **box**, mommy. I'll help you.*

zhè xiē **shíwù** ne fàng zài wánjù chúfáng ma
这些食物呢？放在玩具厨房吗？

And the **food**? In the toy kitchen?

*bù xíng māma yào fàng zài **lánzi** lǐ*
不行、妈妈、要放在篮子里。

*No, mommy, in the **basket**!*

bǎ **yǎnxì de dàojù** fàng zài **guìzi** lǐ
把演戏的道具放在柜子里。

Let's put the **costumes** in the **trunk**.

dōu fàng hǎo le hǎo jí le
都放好了！好极了！

We're done! Yeah!

wáwa
娃娃

shìbīng
士兵

shíwù
食物

yǎnxì de dàojù
演戏的道具

27

bànyǎn xiāofáng yuán
扮演消防员

Playing Firemen

*jǐnglíng xiǎng le **jǐnglíng** xiǎng le*
警铃响了！警铃响了！

*The alarm is ringing! The **alarm** is ringing!*

cóng **huágān** shàng huá xiàlái
从滑竿上滑下来。

Let's go down the **pole**.

chuānshàng nǐde **fánghuǒ yī**
穿上你的防火衣。

Put on your **suit**.

chuān shàng nǐde **xuēzi**
穿上你的靴子.

Put on your **boots**.

dài shàng nǐde **tóukuī**
戴上你的头盔。

Put on your **helmet**.

shàng chē ba zhǔnbèi hǎo le ma
上车吧。准备好了吗？

Get in the truck. Ready?

kuài ràng kāi kuài ràng kāi
快让开！快让开！

Clear the way! Clear the way!

bǎ **jǐngdí** dǎkāi
把警笛打开。

Turn on the **siren**.

zhuā zhù **shuǐguǎn**
抓住水管。

Grab the **hose**.

ràng **shuǐ chōng chūlái**
让水冲出来。

Blast a **stream of water**.

wǎng shàng pá shàng **tīzi**
往上！爬上梯子。

Up! Climb up the **ladder**.

zuò de hǎo
做得好！

Great job!

huǒ xīmiè le
火熄灭了。

The **fire** is out.

xiāofáng yuán
消防员

tóukuī
头盔

shuǐguǎn
水管

shuǐ chōng chūlái
水冲出来

xiāofáng chē
消防车

The Fire Truck

kuài diǎn kuài diǎn
快点！快点！

Hurry! Hurry!

nǐde **tóukuī** zài nǎli
你的头盔在哪里？

Where's your **helmet**?

wǒmen xiànzài jiù qù
我们现在就去！

Let's go now!

tiào shàng **xiāofáng chē**
跳上消防车。

Get in the **fire truck**.

kuài diǎn kuài diǎn
快点！快点！

Hurry! Hurry!

dīng dīng dīng dīng
叮、叮、叮、叮。

Ding, ding, ding, ding.

nàgè **fángzi zháohuǒ** le
那个房子着火了！

There's a **fire** in that **house**!

pá shàng **tīzi**
爬上梯子！

Climb up the **ladder**!

cóng **chuāngzi** jìnqù
从窗子进去。

Get in through the **window**.

shuǐ chōng chūlái lā
水冲出来啦！

Here goes a blast of water!

wǒmen chénggōng le **huǒ** xīmiè le
我们成功了！火熄灭了。

We did it! The **fire** is out.

fángzǐ zháohuǒ
房子着火

xiāofáng chē
消防车

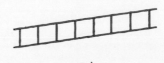

tīzi
梯子

huǒ
火

gōngzhǔ
公主

Princesses

nǐ yào dāng **báixuě gōngzhǔ** ma
你要当白雪公主吗？

Would you like to be **Snow White**?

*bù yào wǒ yào dāng **huīgūniang***
不要、我要当灰姑娘。

*No, I would like to be **Cinderella**.*

hǎo de dài shàng zhè dǐng **huángguān**
好的。戴上这顶皇冠。

Okay. Put on this **crown**.

nǐ dāng **wǔshì** hǎo ma
你当武士、好吗？

And you are the **knight**, okay?

nǐ kàn huīgūniang yǒu yī gè wǔshì
你看、灰姑娘、有一个武士！

Look, Cinderella, a knight!

wǒmen dàshēng jiào
我们大声叫！

Let's scream!

wǒmen zài zhèlǐ zài zhèlǐ wǔshì
我们在这里、在这里武士！

We are here, here knight!

nǐ kàn tā yǒu yī bǎ **jiàn** tā yīdìng huì **jiù wǒmen**
你看！他有一把剑！他一定会救我们。

Look! He has a **sword**! He will **save us**.

Did You Know?

The magnificent complex palace of the Forbidden City in Beijing, also named the Palace Museum, was home to twenty-four emperors who ruled over the country from the Ming Dynasty to the last emperor of the Qing Dynasty in 1912. About thirteen centuries ago, there was a famous princess of the Tang Dynasty named Princess Wencheng (Wénchéng Gōngzhǔ 文成公主). She traveled two thousand miles from the palace in Chang'an to marry the King of Tubo (in today's Tibet). This interracial matrimony helped strengthen the ties between the Tang Dynasty and the Tubo Kingdom. The story of Princess Wencheng has been passed down from generation to generation ever since.

gōngzhǔ
公主

huángguān
皇冠

wǔshì
武士

jiàn
剑

hǎidào
海盗

Pirates

wǒ shì **hǎidào** lán húzi
我是海盗蓝胡子。

I'm the **pirate** Blue Beard.

kàn kàn **dìtú**
看看地图。

Look at the **map**.

bǎozàng zài yī gè **huāngdǎo** shàng
宝藏在一个荒岛上。

The **treasure** is on a **desert island**.

nà shì yī tiáo **chuán** dàjiā shàng chuán
那是一条船。大家上船！

That's the **ship**. All aboard!

kuài diǎn xíngdòng kuài
快点行动！快！

Get moving! Quickly!

hēi gōngzhǔ hǎidào cónglái bù **qīnwěn**
嘿、公主！海盗从来不亲吻！

Hey, princess! Pirates don't **kiss**!

fēng zhēn dà **bàofēngyǔ** jiùyào lái le
风真大！暴风雨就要来了！

What a **wind**! A **storm** is coming!

lùdì lùdì wǒ kāndào le **bǎozàng dǎo**
陆地！陆地！我看到了宝藏岛！

Land! Land! I see the treasure **island**!

bǎ **máo** fàngxià lái
把锚放下来！

Pull down the **anchor**!

tiào jìn huáchuán
跳进划船！

To the rowing boats!

zhuāzhù **chuánjiǎng** kuài kuài huá kuài
抓住船桨快快划。快！

Grab the **paddles** and row. Quick!

dìtú
地图

bǎozàng
宝藏

chuánjiǎng
船桨

máo
锚

zài qìchē xiūlǐ diàn
在汽车修理店

At the Auto Mechanic

qìchē huài le
汽车坏了。

The car doesn't work.

nǐ néng bāng wǒ **xiūlǐ** ma
你能帮我修理吗?

Will you help me **fix** it?

chē zi qǐdòng de shíhòu yǒu qíguài de
zàoyīn
车子启动的时候有奇怪的噪音。

It makes a funny **noise** when it starts.

tīng zhe sī sī sī pū
听着:"嘶嘶嘶噗!"

Listen: "Rrrrr puff!"

*wǒmen lái kànkàn **yǐnqíng** ba*
我们来看看引擎吧!

*Let's look at the **engine**!*

qǐng bǎ **guǎnziqián** dì gěi wǒ
请把管子钳递给我。

Pass me the **monkey wrench**, please.

zhè shì hǎo de
这是好的。

This is fine.

bǎ **dīngchuí** dì gěi wǒ
把钉锤递给我。

Pass me the **hammer**.

zhè gè méi huà
这个没坏。

This is fine.

bǎ **luósīdāo** hé **qiánzi** dì gěi wǒ
把螺丝刀和钳子递给我。

Pass me the **screwdriver** and the **pliers**.

zhè yě dōu búshì
这也都不是。

This isn't it either.

āiyō tiān ā zhè shì shénme
哎哟、天啊! 这是什么?

Oh, boy! And what is this?

Bàba wǒmen jiào xiū chē shīfu ba
爸爸、我们叫修车师傅吧!

Dad, let's call a mechanic!

guǎnziqián
管子钳

dīngchuí
钉锤

luósīdāo
螺丝刀

qiánzi
钳子

zài jiāyóu zhàn
在加油站

At the Gas Station

qǐng jiā mǎn **tèjí yóu**
请加满特级油。

Fill'er up with **super**, please.

yòng **xìnyòngkǎ** háishì **xiànjīn**
用信用卡还是现金？

Credit card or **cash**?

zhè shì xìnyòngkǎ
这是信用卡。

Credit card. Here.

qǐng dǎkāi **yóuxiāng**
请打开油箱。

Open the **tank**, please.

bàba wǒmen lái qīngjié qìchē
爸爸、我们来清洁汽车。

Dad, let's clean the car.

hǎo zhǔyì yáo shàng **chē chuāng**
好主意。关上车窗。

Good idea. Close the **(car) windows**.

yòng gèngduō de **féizào** bǎ **chēlún** hǎo
    hǎo cā yī cā
用更多的肥皂。把车轮好好擦一擦。

Wipe the **wheels** well. With more **soap**.

bǎ **fāngxiàngpán** yě cā yī cā
把方向盘也擦一擦。

Wipe the **steering wheel** as well.

xiànzài kāi **xīchénqì** bǎ **zuòwèi** xī yī xī
    hǎo lā quánbù wánchéng
现在开吸尘器把座位吸一吸。好啦、全部
    完成！

Now run the **vacuum cleaner** over the **seats**.
    All done!

xìnyòngkǎ
信用卡

xiànjīn
现金

chē chuāng
车窗

fāngxiàngpán
方向盘

zuò yùndòng
做运动 Playing Sports

tīzúqiú
踢足球

Playing Soccer

wǒmen gēn nǐde **péngyoumen** yiqi tī **zúqiú** ba
我们跟你的朋友们一起踢足球吧！

Let's play **soccer** with your **friends**!

wǒmen xūyào yī gè **qiú** hé yī gè **wǎng**
我们需要一个球和一个网。

We need a **ball** and a **net**.

*dàwèi shì **shǒumén yuán***
大卫是守门员。

*David is the **goalie**.*

wǒmen bǎ qiú tī dào tā nàr dé fēn ba
我们把球踢到他那儿得分吧。

Let's score a goal on him.

lái ba kuài pǎo chuán **qiú**
来吧、快跑、传球。

Come on, run, pass the **ball**.

jìn qiú jìn qiú lā
进球！进球啦！

Goal! Gooooooooal!

xiànzài nǐ shì **shǒumén yuán**
现在你是守门员。

Now you are the **goalie**.

qù zhàn zài wǎng nàbiān
去站在网那边。

Go to the net.

qiú chūjiè le
球出界了！

Out of bounds!

*lái tī yī gè **jiǎo qiú***
来踢一个角球。

*Make a **corner kick**.*

*yòng nǐde **tóu** dǐng qiú*
用你的头顶球。

*Hit it with your **head**.*

lái ba kuài pǎo chuán qiú
来吧、快跑、传球。

Come on, run, pass the ball.

wǒmen zài jìn qiú dé fēn ba
我们再进球得分吧！

Let's score another goal!

zúqiú
足球

wǎng
网

shǒumén yuán
守门员

qiú chūjiè
球出界

yīqǐ lái tiào shéng
一起来跳绳

shéngzi lūn de tuán tuán zhuǎn
绳子抡的团团转、
mèimei jìnlái tiào tiào kàn
妹妹进来跳跳看。
yī èr sān sì wǔ liù qī
一、二、三、四、五、六、七。
tiào de guò de jìn nǐ **wán**
跳得过的尽你玩。
yī èr sān **sì wǔ liù qī**
一、二、三、四、五、六、七。
tiào búguò de jiù yào **huàn**
跳不过的就要换。

Let's Jump Rope

The **rope** whirling round and round,

little **sister** came to jump rope.

One, **two**, **three**, four, five, six, seven.

If you can **jump**, **play** as long as you want.

One, two, three, **four**, **five**, **six**, **seven**.

If you can't jump, **change** the players.

Did You Know?

Chinese jump rope is a fun twist on traditional jump roping games. To play, two children attach long elastic ropes or bands (xiàngpí jīn 橡皮筋) to their ankles. Other children jump in, out, and around the ropes in a game that resembles a hybrid of Double Dutch and Hopscotch. The game originated in seventh century China. When you play Chinese jump rope, you can develop eye and foot coordination, and, of course, have fun with your friends!

shéngzi
绳子

tiào
跳

mèimei
妹妹

yī èr sān
一二三

qù de dìfāng
去的地方　　Going Places

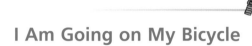

wǒ qí zhe wǒde zìxíngchē
我骑着我的自行车

I Am Going on My Bicycle

dài shàng nǐde **tóukuī**
戴上你的头盔。

Put on your **helmet**.

wǒmen jīngguò **gōngyuán**
我们经过公园。

We are going through the **park**.

wǒmen qí **màn** yīdiǎn
我们骑慢一点。

Let's go **slowly**.

*wǒ qí zhe **zìxíngchē** chuān guò gōngyuán*
我骑着自行车穿过公园。

*I'm riding my **bike** through the park.*

xiànzài zài mǎlù shàng wǒmen qí **kuài yīdiǎn**
现在在马路上。我们骑快一点。

Now on the road. Let's go **quickly**.

*zài **mǎlù** shàng wǒ qí zhe wǒde zìxíngchē*
在马路上我骑着我的自行车。

*I'm riding my bike on the **road**.*

xiànzài zài **cǎodì** shàng gāogāo dīdī duōme **bù píng**
现在在草地上。高高低低多么不平！

Now in the **field**. It's so **bumpy**!

*zài **cǎodì** shàng wǒ qí zhe wǒde zìxíngchē*
在草地上我骑着我的自行车。

*I'm riding my bike in the **field**.*

wǒmen yīqǐ shàng **shān** ba
我们一起上山吧！

Let's go up the **mountain**!

***wǎng shàng** wǎng shàng wǎng shàng qí
wǎng xià wǎng xià wǎng xià qí*
往上、往上、往上骑、往下、往下、往下骑！

***Up**, up, up, and down, down, **down**!*

tóukuī
头盔

mǎlù
马路

cǎodì
草地

shān
山

36

hónglǜdēng
红绿灯

The Traffic Light

kòu shàng **ānquándài** wǒmen zǒu 扣上安全带 - 我们走！	Buckle your **belt**–and we go!
lǜdēng **lǜdēng** 绿灯！绿灯！	Green light! **Green light**!
wǒ gāi zěnmebàn 我该怎么办？	What do I do?
*kāi kuài diǎn kāi kuài diǎn kāi **kuài** diǎn* 开快点、开快点、开快点。	*Go fast, fast, **fast***.
bì bì dū dū 哗、哗！嘟、嘟！	*Beep, beep! Honk, honk!*
huáng dēng **huáng dēng** 黄灯！黄灯！	Yellow light! **Yellow light**!
wǒ gāi zěnmebàn 我该怎么办？	What do I do?
kāi màn diǎn kāi màn diǎn kāi de fēicháng màn 开慢点、开慢点、开得非常慢。	*Go slowly, slowly, very **slowly***.
hóng dēng **hóng dēng** wǒ gāi zěnmebàn 红灯！红灯！我该怎么办？	Red light! **Red light**! What do I do?
tíngxià lái 停下来！	*Stop!*

qìchē
汽车

lǜdēng
绿灯

huáng dēng
黄灯

hóng dēng
红灯

wǒmen qù gōngyuán wán

我们去公园玩! Let's Go to the Park!

zài gōngyuán lǐ
在公园里

In the Park

nǐ yàobúyào liū **huátī**

你要不要溜滑梯?

Would you like to go on the **slide**?

shǒu zhuājǐn le **huá xiàqù**

手抓紧了滑下去!

Hold on tight and **go down**!

nǐ yào bú yào qù wán **dāngàng**

你要不要去玩单杠?

Would you like to go to the **monkey bars**?

hǎo a yī èr sān sì wǔ liù qī bā
bā gēn gàng zi

好啊! 一、二、三、四、五、六、七、
八。八根杠子!

Yes! One, two, three, four, five, six, seven, eight.
Eight bars up!

nǐ yào bú yào qù shàng **tǎlóu**

你要不要去上塔楼?

Would you like to go to the **tower**?

dāngrán yào yī èr sān sì wǔ liù qī bā jiǔ
shí shí-yī shí-èr

当然要! 一、二、三、四、五、六、七、
八、九、十、十一、十二。

Sure! One, two, three, four, five, six, seven, eight,
nine, ten, eleven, twelve.

Did You Know?

Many public parks in China have an amusement area for children. Grannies and nannies bring children to play in the parks. In the parks, there are all kinds of activities for people of all ages. In the morning, it's very common to see people exercising. They practice the slow movements of Tai Chi, or dance (with or without music). Some people exercise individually, while some exercise in groups of three, four, or even dozens of people. Another activity that occurs in Chinese parks is the practice of "walking birds," which is when old men bring birds in cages and gather under trees to chat and listen to the birds singing. Other activities enjoyed in the parks are listening to Chinese opera, playing traditional Chinese instruments, playing Chinese chess, or drinking tea together.

gōngyuán
公园

huátī
滑梯

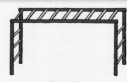

dāngàng
单杠

tǎlóu
塔楼

dàng qiūqiān
荡秋千

On the Swings

wǒmen qù dàng **qiūqiān** ba
我们去荡秋千吧。

Let's go to the **swings**.

yào wǒ tuī nǐ ma jiù zhèyàng
要我推你吗？就这样！

Shall I push you? There you go!

yònglì tuī
用力推！

Harder!

nǐ wèishénme bù zìjǐ tuī ne
你为什么不自己推呢？

Why don't you push yourself?

bǎ nǐde **tuǐ** yònglì xiàng qián shēn
把你的腿用力向前伸。

Pump your **legs** forward.

zài bǎ tuǐ yònglì wǎng hòu wān
再把腿用力往后弯。

Now pump your legs back.

jiù nàyàng **wǎng qián wǎng hòu**
就那样、往前、往后。

Like that, **forward**, **back**.

nǐ yào bú yào tíngxiàlái
你要不要停下来？

Do you want to stop?

*hǎo a wǒ xiǎng qù zuò **qiāoqiāo bǎn***
好啊！我想去坐跷跷板。

*Yes! I want to go to the **seesaw**.*

dōu zuò mǎn le wǒmen děi děng yī děng
都坐满了。我们得等一等。

It's full. We'll have to wait.

nǐ è le ma zhèr yǒu **huǒtuǐ sānmíngzhì**
你饿了吗？这儿有火腿三明治。

Are you hungry? There's a **ham sandwich**.

qiūqiān
秋千

qiāoqiāo bǎn
跷跷板

sānmíngzhì
三明治

huǒtuǐ
火腿

wǒmen qù hǎowán de dìfāng

我们去好玩的地方！ Let's Go to Fun Places!

zài dòngwùyuán
在动物园

At the Zoo

shīzi huì jiào hǒu hǒu hǒu
狮子会叫、"吼吼吼。"

The lions say, "Grrrrr."

gōng shīzi yǒu **zōngmáo mǔshīzi** méiyǒu
公狮子有鬃毛、母狮子没有。

The lion has a **mane** and the **lioness** doesn't.

shīzi zài shuìjiào
狮子在睡觉。

The **lion** is sleeping.

nǐ kàn **chángjǐnglù**
你看、长颈鹿！

Look, the **giraffes**!

*tāmen de **jǐngzi** duōme cháng*
他们的颈子多么长！

*What long **necks** they have!*

dàxiàng *yǒu dà ěrduo*
大象有大耳朵！

*The **elephants** have big **ears**!*

kàn tāmen yòng **bízi** ná huāshēng
看他们用鼻子拿花生。

Look how they get the peanuts with their **trunk**.

*wǒ kāndào **lǎohǔ** yǒu hǎo dà de **yáchǐ***
我看到老虎！有好大的牙齿！

*I see the **tigers**! What large **teeth**!*

kàn kàn **shé** tāmen shuō sī sī sī
看看蛇！他们说、"嘶嘶嘶。"

Look at the **snakes**! They say, "Sssss."

*zhè yī tiáo zhēn **cháng***
这一条真长！

*This one is so **long**!*

Did You Know?

Mandarin Chinese is one of the six official languages of the United Nations. It is mostly spoken in mainland China, Hong Kong, Taiwan, and Singapore. The Chinese language does not have an alphabet and is written in characters. Pinyin is a way to spell the sounds of Mandarin Chinese with the Roman alphabet. Chinese characters represent one of the oldest writing systems in the world.

shīzi
狮子

chángjǐnglù
长颈鹿

dàxiàng
大象

lǎohǔ
老虎

zài yóulèyuán
在游乐园

At the Amusement Park

nǐ xiǎng zuò shénme **yóulèshèshi**
你想坐什么游乐设施？

Which **ride** do you want to go on?

*zuò **mótiānlún***
坐摩天轮。

*On the **Ferris wheel**.*

hǎo de wǒmen qù mǎi **piào**
好的。我们去买票。

Okay. Let's buy the **tickets**.

bǎ piào gěi tā ránhòuzuò zài zhèr
把票给他、然后坐在这儿。

Give the ticket to him, and sit here.

*wǒ xiànzài xiǎng zuò **xuánzhuǎn mùmǎ lún***
我现在想坐旋转木马轮！

*I want to go on the **merry-go-round** now!*

wǒ huì bǎ nǐ bào qǐlai zuò zài **mǎ** bèi shàng
我会把你抱起来坐在马背上。

I'll get you up on the **horse**.

nǐ xiànzài xiǎng wán shénme
你现在想玩什么？

Where would you like to go now?

*qù wán **pèngpèng chē** wǒ kāichē*
去玩碰碰车。我开车！

*To the **bumper cars**. I'll drive!*

kuài pǎo wǒmen qù zuò hóngsè de qìchē
块跑、我们去坐红色的汽车。

Run, let's go to the red car.

*zuò **yúnxiāo fēichē** de shíjiān dào le*
坐云霄飞车的时间到了！

*Time for the **roller coaster**!*

mótiānlún
摩天轮

xuánzhuǎn mùmǎ
旋转木马

pèngpèng chē
碰碰车

yúnxiāo fēichē
云霄飞车

qù kàn qīnqi
去看亲戚 Visiting Family

qù kàn nǎinai hé yéye
去看奶奶和爷爷

Going to Grandma and Grandpa's

wǒmen qù **yéye nǎinai jiā**
我们去爷爷奶奶家。

We are going to **grandma and grandpa's house**.

shì tāmende **jiéhūn jìniàn rì**
是他们的结婚纪念日。

It's their **anniversary**.

wǒmen dǎsuàn chī jiǎozǐ zhēn hǎo chī
我们打算吃饺子。真好吃！

We are going to eat dumplings. How delicious!

wǒmen dào le xià **chē** ba
我们到了！下车吧。

We arrived! Get out of the **car**.

qīnqīn bàobào nǎinai
亲亲抱抱奶奶。

Give your grandma a **kiss** and a **hug**.

wǒ ài nǐ
我爱你。

I love you.

Did You Know?

Chinese families refer to one another by their kinship. Birth order is one factor. For example, jiějiě 姐姐 means older sister, gēgē 哥哥 means older brother, mèimei 妹妹 means younger sister, and dìdì 弟弟 means younger brother. Another factor is maternal and paternal lineage. Your paternal grandfather is called yéye 爷爷 and your paternal grandmother is nǎinai 奶奶. Your maternal grandfather is wàigōng 外公 and your maternal grandmother is wàipó 外婆. An "uncle" can refer to your father's older brother bóbo 伯伯 or younger brother shūshu 叔叔. The brothers on your mother's side are all called jiùjiu 舅舅. An "aunt" can refer to your father's sisters gūgu 姑姑 or your mother's sisters āyí 阿姨. The children of your father's brothers are táng cousins táng xiōngdì jiěmèi 堂兄弟姐妹 and they share the same surname with you. The cousins who do not share the same surname are biǎo cousins biǎo xiōngdì jiěmèi 表兄弟姐妹.

yéye hé nǎinai
爷爷和奶奶

jiùjiu hé āyí
舅舅和阿姨

biǎo xiōngdì jiěmèi
表兄弟姐妹

bàba hé māma
爸爸和妈妈

wǒde jiātíng
我的家庭

My Family

wǒmen lái kànkàn **zhàoxiàng běn**
我们来看看照相本。

Let's look at the **album**.

nǐ zhībùzhīdào zhè shì shéi
你知不知道这是谁？

Do you know who this is?

*bùzhī dào shì wǒde **shūshū** ma*
不知道。是我的叔叔吗？

*No idea. Is he my **uncle**?*

tā shì **yéye** zhè shì tā xiǎo **nánhái** de shíhòu
他是爷爷、这是他小男孩的时候。

It's **grandpa**, when he was a little **boy**.

wǒ juédé nǐ zhǎng de zhēn xiàng tā
我觉得你长得真像他！

I think you look just like him!

bù kěnéng tā chuān zhe shénme
不可能！他穿着什么？

No way! What is he wearing?

èn shì nà gè shíhòu tāmen chuān de yīfu
嗯、是那个时候他们穿的衣服。

Well, that's how they dressed back then.

zhè shì **nǎinai** hé tāde **jiěmèi**
这是奶奶和她的姐妹。

And this is **grandma** and her **sisters**.

tāmen dōu shì nǚshēng
她们都是女生！

They are all girls!

wǒ zhīdào nǐ bù xǐhuān **nǚshēng**
我知道！你不喜欢女生。

I know! You don't like **girls**.

nánshēng bǐjiào hǎo wán ma
男生比较好玩嘛！

Boys are much more fun!

jiātíng
家庭

bàobào
抱抱

nánhái
男孩

nǚshēng
女生

dòngwù
动物 Animals

zài nóngchǎng
在农场

At the Farm

wǒmen qù kàn **mǔjī**
我们去看母鸡。

Let's look at the **hens**.

mǔjī shuō gūgū gūgū gūgū
母鸡说、"咕咕、咕咕、咕咕。"

The hens say, "Cluck, cluck, cluck."

huǒjī shuō gēgē tà gēgē tà gēgē tà
火鸡说、"咯咯嗒、咯咯嗒、咯咯嗒。"

The **turkeys** say, "Gobble, gobble, gobble."

nǐ kàn **gōngjī** zài wūdǐng shàng
你看、公鸡在屋顶上！

Look, the **rooster** is up on the roof!

gōngjī shuō yī wō wō wō wō
公鸡说、"咿喔喔喔喔！"

The rooster says, "cock-a-doodle-doo!"

xiǎo jī shuō jījī jījī jījī
小鸡说、"唧唧、唧唧、唧唧。"

The **chicks** say, "peep, peep, peep."

nǐ xiǎng kàn **niú** ma
你想看牛吗？

Do you want to see the **cows**?

nǐ kàn **xiǎo niú** zài chī nǎi
你看、小牛在吃奶。

Look, the little **calf** is nursing.

Did You Know?

There are more than a hundred wild animal species unique to China, including well-known rare animals such as the black-and-white giant panda, golden-haired monkeys, brown-eared pheasants, red-crowned cranes, white South China tigers, red ibises, white-flag dolphins and Chinese alligators. The dragon is a traditional animal symbol often associated with the emperor, and the phoenix with the empress. In the Chinese zodiac, each year of the twelve-year cycle is represented by a different animal. People who are born in the year of a certain animal are said to exhibit certain personality traits unique to the animal sign. The twelve zodiac animals are the rat (lǎoshǔ 老鼠), ox (niú 牛), tiger (lǎohǔ 老虎), rabbit (tù zǐ 兔子), dragon (lóng 龙), snake (shé 蛇), horse (mǎ 马), sheep (yáng 羊), monkey (hóuzi 猴子), rooster (jī 鸡), dog (gǒu 狗), and pig (zhū 猪).

nóngchǎng
农场

mǔjī
母鸡

mǎ
马

niú
牛

dòngwù dōu zài wán
动物都在玩

The Animals Play

xiǎo **niǎo** zài kōngzhōng fēixiáng
小鸟在空中飞翔、
fēi fēi fēi fēi fēi
飞、飞、飞、飞、飞。
xiǎo **yú** zài shuǐ zhōng yóuyǒng
小鱼在水中游泳、
yóu yóu yóu yóu yóu
游、游、游、游、游。
xiǎo **mǎ** zài shān shàng pǎobù
小马在山上跑步、
pǎo pǎo pǎo pǎo pǎo
跑、跑、跑、跑、跑。
xiǎo **tùzǐ** zài cǎodì shàng tiào
小兔子在草地上跳、
tiào tiào tiào tiào tiào
跳、跳、跳、跳、跳。
xiǎo **sōngshǔ** zài shù shàng pá
小松鼠在树上爬、
pá pá pá pá pá
爬、爬、爬、爬、爬。

The little **birds** that go by the air,

fly, fly, fly, fly, fly.

The little **fish** that go by the water,

swim, swim, swim, swim, swim.

The little **horses** that go by the mountain,

run, run, run, run, run.

The little **rabbits** that go by the field,

jump, jump, jump, jump, jump.

The little **squirrels** that go by the tree,

climb, climb, climb, climb, climb.

niǎo
鸟

yú
鱼

tùzi
兔子

sōngshǔ
松鼠

wǒ bù shūfu
我不舒服　　　I Don't Feel Well

qù kàn yīshēng
去看医生

To the Doctor's

à nǐ **késòu** le
啊！你咳嗽了！

Oh! What a **cough**!

bǎ nǐde **zuǐba** zhāngkāi zhāng dà yīdiǎn
把你的嘴巴张开，张大一点。

Open your **mouth** wide, wider.

dàshēng shuō ā ā ā ā
大声说 "啊啊啊啊。"

Say "ahhhhhh" very **loud**.

nǐde **hóulong** fāyán le
你的喉咙发炎了。

Your **throat** is inflamed.

nǐde **ěrduo** téng ma ràng wǒ kànkàn zhè zhī
　　ěrduo
你的耳朵疼吗？让我看看这只耳朵。

Do your **ears** hurt? Let me see this ear.

ò à zhè yī zhī fāyán le
哦、啊！这一只发炎了！

Oh, oh! This one is infected!

liú bítì le lái ná **shǒujīn zhǐ**
流鼻涕了！来拿手巾纸。

What a **runny nose**! Here, a **tissue**.

bǎ **wēndùjì** fàng jìn zuǐ lǐ
把温度计放进嘴里。

Put in the **thermometer**.

nǐ **fāshāo** le
你发烧了。

You have a **fever**.

hē yī **tāngchí** de **yàoshuǐ**
喝一汤匙的药水

Take a **tablespoon** of this **syrup**

yītiān liǎng cì hái yào hē hěnduō shuǐ
一天两次、还要喝很多水。

two times a day, and drink a lot of water.

yī gè xīngqī hòu zài lái kàn nǐ hěn kuài jiù
　　huì hǎo de
一个星期后再来看。你很快就会好的！

Come back in a week. Get well!

hóulong
喉咙

ěrduo
耳朵

bítì
鼻涕

hóng bízi
红鼻子

gǎnmào
感冒

The Cold

chī yào de shíjiān dào le
吃药的时间到了。

It's time to take the medicine.

niē zhù nǐde **bízi** kuài bǎ yào tūn xiàqù
捏住你的鼻子快把药吞下去。

Pinch your **nose** and swallow it quickly.

cái búyào zhēn ě xīn
才不要！真恶心！

No way! It's disgusting!

a jiū a jiū
啊啾！啊啾！

Achoo! Achoo!

zhèyàng huì bāng nǐ juédé shūfu yīdiǎn
这样会帮你觉得舒服一点。

It would help you feel better.

wǒ xǐhuān shēngbìng dāi zài jiā lǐ
我喜欢生病呆在家里。

I like being sick and staying at home.

ò wǒ míngbai le dànshì wú lǎoshī huì hěn
xiǎng nǐ nǐ shì tā zuì xǐhuān de
xuésheng
哦、我明白了！但是吴老师会很想你，你
是她最喜欢的学生 . . .

Oh, I see! But then Ms. Woods will miss
you. You are her favorite **student** . . .

*èn zhè shì zhēnde yěxǔ **míngtiān** wǒ jiù
kěyǐ qù shàngxué le*
嗯、这是真的。也许明天我就可以去上学
了。

*Well, that's true. Maybe I could go
tomorrow.*

wēndùjì
温度计

tāngchí
汤匙

yàoshuǐ
药水

yǎnjīng yǒu yǎnlèi
眼睛有眼泪

shēngrì kuàilè
生日快乐!   Happy Birthday!

shēngrì pàiduì
生日派对

The Birthday Party

nǐ jǐ suì le
你几岁了？

How old are you?

liù suì
六岁！

Six!

ò tiān na nǐ zhème lǎo le
哦、天哪！你这么老了！

Oh, my! You are so old!

èn **shēngrì kuàilè** lǎo shòu xīng
嗯、生日快乐、老寿星！

Well, **happy birthday**, old fellow!

zài zhèlǐ shì nǐde **lǐwù** bǎ tā dǎkāi
在这里、是你的礼物。把它打开。

Here, your **gift**. Open it.

*shì yī jià **zhíshēng fēijī***
是一架直升飞机！

*It's a **helicopter**!*

zhè yī bāo yě shì bǎ tā dǎkāi
这一包也是！把它打开。

And this too! Open it.

*zhè shì yī tiáo **hǎidào chuán***
这是一条海盗船！

*It's a **pirate boat**!*

háizimen chī dàngāo le
孩子们、吃蛋糕了！

Kids, the cake!

Did You Know?

While it is becoming more popular in China to have children's birthday parties, the birthday celebrations for newborns and elderly people are still more important and elaborate. Sons and daughters throw big banquets for their elderly parents' birthdays to show their respect and express gratitude. When a child is one month old, it is customary for the family to invite friends and relatives to dinner and offer them red-colored eggs. Children usually receive gifts such as a longevity lock or money in a red envelope for good luck. Typical presents for elderly people are paintings or craftwork with cypress trees, red-crowned cranes, or characters symbolizing longevity and good wishes.

lǐwù
礼物

zhíshéng fēijī
直升飞机

chuán
船

hǎidào
海盗

dàngāo
蛋糕

The Cake

dàngāo zhǔnbèi hǎo le
蛋糕准备好了！

The **cake** is ready!

měi gè rén dōu guòlái zhèlǐ
每个人、都过来这里！

Everybody, come here!

qǐng guān **dēng**
请关灯！

Turn off the **lights**, please!

wǒmen lái chànggē yī èr sān
我们来唱歌。一、二、三。

Let's sing. One, two, and three.

zhù nǐ shēngrì kuàilè
祝你生日快乐 . . .

Happy birthday to you . . .

xǔ yī gè yuànwàng ránhòu chuīxī **làzhú**
许一个愿望，然后吹熄蜡烛。

Make a wish and blow out the **candles**.

hǎo shéi yào dàngāo
好！谁要蛋糕？

Good! Who wants cake?

nǐ yào **qiǎokèlì** dàngāo ma
你要巧克力蛋糕吗？

Do you want some **chocolate** cake?

yào wǒ xǐhuān qiǎokèlì
要。我喜欢巧克力。

Yes. I love chocolate.

nǐ yào yī **dà kuài** de háishi yī **xiǎo kuài**
de dàngāo
你要一大块的还是一小块的蛋糕？

Would you like a **big** or a **small piece**?

shēngrì dàngāo
生日蛋糕

làzhú
蜡烛

dà kuài
一大块

xiǎo kuài
一小块

zài hǎitān
在海滩

At the Beach

shāzi shì rè de
沙子是热的！

The sand is hot!

nà jiù bú yào tuō diào nǐde **liángxié**
那就不要脱掉你的凉鞋！

Don't take off your **sandals** then!

děng yī děng bié zǒukāi guòlái
等一等！别走开。过来！

Wait! Don't go away. Come here!

wǒ bāng nǐ cā **fángshài shuāng**
我帮你擦防晒霜。

I'll put some **sunscreen** on you.

wǒ bù yào ràng nǐ bèi tàiyáng shài jiāo
我不要让你被太阳晒焦。

I don't want you to get burned.

wǒ kěyǐ jiè yòng yīxià nǐde **chǎnzi** ma
我可以借用一下你的铲子吗？

Can I borrow your **shovel** for a moment?

wǒ lái wā yī gè kěyǐ bǎ **sǎn** chā jìnqù de dòng
我来挖一个可以把伞插进去的洞。

I'll dig a hole for the **umbrella**.

*wǒ xiǎng qù **shuǐ** lǐ wán*
我想去水里玩！

*I want to go in the **water**!*

hǎo de dài shàng nǐde **jiùshēng quān**
好的。戴上你的救生圈。

Okay. Put on your **inner tube**.

Did You Know?

You can set up a "beach" in the playroom or the backyard. Make a sun with construction paper. Mark off a pretend swimming area with tape. You can make a sandbox with a large container filled with sand and toys. Use a beach bag with beach towels, sand toys, and sunscreen. Have fun!

liángxié
凉鞋

fángshài shuāng
防晒霜

sǎn
伞

jiùshēng quān
救生圈

shā chéngbǎo
沙城堡

Sand Castles

hēi bú yào rēng shāzi
嘿！不要扔沙子！

Hey! Don't throw sand!

lái ba wǒmen gài yī gè **shā chéngbǎo** ba
来吧。我们盖一个沙城堡吧。

Come on. Let's make a **sand castle**.

zhè shì **tǒngzi** hé **chǎnzi**
这是桶子和铲子。

Here is the **bucket** and the **shovel**.

bǎ tǒngzi lǐ zhuāng mǎn **shāzi**
把桶子里装满沙子。

Fill the bucket with **sand**.

ránhòu bǎ tǒngzi fān guòlái qīngqīng de
    pāi dǎ
然后把桶子翻过来,轻轻地拍打。

Now flip it over and pat it softly.

bǎ tǒngzi ná qǐlai mànmàn de ná
把桶子拿起来。慢慢地拿！

Now lift the bucket. Slowly!

*wǒ hái xiǎng gài gèngduō de **chéngbǎo***
我还想盖更多的城堡。

*I want to make more **towers**.*

hǎo ba wǒ yòng **pázi** zuò tiáo **xiǎo lù**
好吧、我用耙子做条小路。

All right, I'll make a **path** with the **rake**.

*wǒmen qù zhǎo **bèiké** lái zhuāngshì
    chéngbǎo*
我们去找贝壳来装饰城堡。

*Let's look for **shells** to decorate the
    castle.*

hǎo ā zhēn shì gè hǎo zhǔyì
好啊！真是个好主意！

Yes! Excellent idea!

shā chéngbǎo
沙城堡

tǒngzi
桶子

chǎnzi
铲子

pázi
耙子

wǒ huì yòng kējì
我会用科技
I Use Technology

wǒmen zài liǎnshū zhāngtiē zhàopiàn
我们在脸书张贴照片

Let's Post Pictures on Facebook

nǐ kěyǐ xuǎn shí zhāng nǐ zuì xǐhuān de
shēngrì **zhàopiàn**
你可以选十张你最喜欢的生日照片。

You can choose your ten favorite **pictures** of your birthday.

nǐ xǐhuān nǎ xiē
你喜欢哪些?

Which ones do you like?

*wǒ xǐhuān wǒ bǎ **dàngāo** diào dào dìshàng
de nà zhāng*
我喜欢我把蛋糕掉到地上的那张。

*I like the one when I dropped the **cake**.*

*yě xǐhuān wǒ ná wǒde **tuītǔjī** de nà zhāng*
也喜欢我拿我的推土机的那张。

*The one with my **bulldozer** too.*

nǐ kàn **nǎinai huífù** le
你看! 奶奶回复了。

Look! **Grandma** posted a **reply**.

tā shuō wǒ hǎo xǐhuān nà jià **fēijī** shì **shéi**
gěi nǐ de
她说、"我好喜欢那架飞机! 是谁给你
的?"

She says, "I love that **airplane**! **Who** gave you that?"

*gàosu tā shì **Jiékè** sònggěi wǒ de*
告诉她是杰克送给我的。

*Say that **Jack** gave it to me.*

yéye shuō tā xiǎngyào wán nǐde
tuītǔjī
爷爷说他想要玩你的推土机。

Grandpa says that he wants to play with your bulldozer.

zhàopiàn
照片

tuītǔjī
推土机

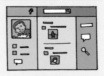
liǎnshū
脸书

dǎkāi
打开

gēn biǎojiě jiǎnghuà
跟表姐讲话

We Talk with Our Cousin

nǐ xiǎngyào gēn nǐde **biǎojiě** jiǎnghuà ma
你想要跟你的表姐讲话吗？

Do you want to talk with your **cousin**?

dāngrán yào
当然要！

Sure!

nà nǐ bǎ **bǐjìběn diànnǎo** ná guòlái gěi wǒ
那你把笔记本电脑拿过来给我。

Then pass me the **laptop**.

wǒ lái dǎkāi diànnǎo wǒ zhīdào zěnme yòng Skype
我来打开电脑！我知道怎么用Skype。

I'll turn it on! I know how to use Skype.

āyí nín hǎo nǐmen zài nǎli
阿姨,您好！你们在哪里？

*Hello, **Aunt**! Where are you?*

zài **gōngyuán** lǐ nǐ xiǎng gēn nǐde biǎojiě jiǎnghuà ma
在公园里。你想跟你的表姐讲话吗？

At the **park**. Do you want to talk with your cousin?

yào a wǒ xiǎng gēn tā jiǎnghuà
要啊、我想跟她讲话。

Yes, I want to talk with her.

bú yào àn nà gè jiàn
不要按那个键！

Don't touch that button!

ài wǒmende wǎngxiàn duàn le
哎！我们的网线断了。

Agh! We lost the connection.

Nǐ kěyǐ bǎ **suíshēntīng** ná chūlái
你可以把随身听拿出来。

You can take out your **iPod**.

bǐjìběn diànnǎo
笔记本电脑

biǎojiě
表姐

āyí
阿姨

suíshēntīng
随身听

53

zài zhōngguó chéng guò xīn nián

在中国城过新年

New Year's in Chinatown

bàba nà shì shénme
爸爸、那是什么？

Dad, what's that?

nà shì qìngzhù zhōngguó xīnnián de wǔ **lóng** yóuxíng zài nàr háiyǒu wǔ **shī**
那是庆祝中国新年的舞龙游行、在那儿还有舞狮。

It's a **dragon** parade for the Chinese New Year, and that over there is a **lion** dance.

qiān zhù wǒ de **shǒu**
牵住我的手。

Hold my **hand** tight.

zhèlǐ de **rén** tài duō le
这里的人太多了。

There are too many **people**.

nà shì shénme **shēngyīn**
那是什么声音？

What's that noise?

shì wǔlóng de dǎ **gǔ** shēngyīn
是舞龙的打鼓声音。

People playing the **drums** for the Dragon Dance.

wǒ xiǎo de shíhòu zài zhōngguó guònián wǒ bàba māma gěi wǒ **hóngbāo** lǐmiàn yǒu **qián**
我小的时候在中国过年、我爸爸妈妈给我红包里面有钱。

When I was little in China, my parents gave me a **red envelope** with **money** for the New Year.

dàibiǎo zhùfú xīnnián **hǎoyùn** de yìsi
代表祝福新年好运的意思。

It means **good luck** for the new year.

wǒ xǐ huān wǒ néng bù néng yǒu hóngbāo
我喜欢！我能不能有红包？

I like that! Can I have one?

wǒ yào yǒu **hǎo duō hǎo duō** *de hǎo yùn*
我要有好多好多的好运气。

*I want **lots and lots** of good luck.*

lóng
龙

gǔ
鼓

hóngbāo
红包

qián
钱

zài chéng lǐ chī dōngxī
在城里吃东西

Eating in the City

*wǒ è le xiàn zài kě yǐ **chī** dōngxi ma*
我饿了。现在可以吃东西吗!

*I'm hungry. I want **to eat** now!*

yǒu lāomiàn bǐsàbǐng **hànbǎobāo** sānmíngzhì
有捞面、比萨饼、汉堡包、三明治 . . .

There's **noodles**, pizza, **hamburgers**, sandwiches . . .

*wǒ yào chī **bǐsàbǐng***
我要吃比萨饼。

*I want **pizza**.*

nǐ yào **hē** shénme hē **shuǐ**
你要喝什么? 喝水?

And what do you want **to drink**? **Water**?

*bú yào yào **kělè***
不要。要可乐。

*No. **Coke**.*

nǐ xiànzài xiǎng zuò shénme
你现在想做什么?

What would you like to do now?

wǒmen qù zuò **shuāng céng bāshì** hǎo ma
我们去坐双层巴士好吗?

Why don't we ride a **double-decker bus**?

bāshì zhàn zài nàr
巴士站在那儿。

The **bus stop** is there.

xíng a kuài pǎo bāshì lái le
行啊。快跑、巴士来了!

Okay. Run, the bus is coming!

shuǐ
水

shuǐguǒ
水果

hànbǎobāo
汉堡包

shuāng céng bāshì
双层巴士

kāixué de dì yī tiān
开学的第一天

The First Day of School

xiǎopéngyǒu nǐ hǎo nǐ jiào shénme míngzi
小朋友你好、你叫什么名字？

Hello, little friend, what's your name?

Wáng Lìlì
王丽丽。

Lily Wang.

Lìlì **huānyíng** wǒ shì Gāo lǎoshī
丽丽、欢迎！我是高老师。

Hi, Lily! **Welcome!** I'm Miss Gao.

xiànzài dàjiā dōu dào qí le wéi chéng yī gè **yuánquān** zuò xià
现在大家都到齐了，围成一个圆圈坐下。

Now that we are all here, let's sit in a **circle**.

jīntiān wǒmen lái shuō yī shuō wǒmen zuì xǐhuān de dōngxī
今天我们来说一说我们最喜欢的东西。

Today we are going to talk about our favorite things.

nǐmen néng cāi yī cai wǒ xǐhuān shénme **yánsè** ma
你们能猜一猜我喜欢什么颜色吗？

Can you guess my favorite **color**?

lán sè hóng sè huáng sè chéng sè
蓝色！红色！黄色！橙色！

Blue! Red! Yellow! Orange!

èn dōu bú duì wǒ xǐhuān **zǐ sè**
嗯都不对。我喜欢紫色！

Nope. It's **purple**!

xiànzài **lún dào nǐ** gàosu dàjiā nǐ zuì xǐhuān shénme **wánjù**
现在轮到你告诉大家你最喜欢什么玩具。

Now **it's your turn** to tell us about your favorite **toys**.

Lín Wěi nǐ zuì xǐhuān de **wánjù** shì shénme
林伟、你最喜欢的玩具是什么？

Lin Wei, which is your favorite **toy**?

lán sè
蓝色

hóng sè
红色

huáng sè
黄色

chéng sè
橙色

wǒmen zuò suànshù
我们做算术！

Let's Do Math!

tóngxuémen zǎoshàng hǎo jīntiān wǒmen
    yīqǐ lái shǔ **shù**

同学们、早上好！今天我们一起来数数。

wǒmen bān yǒu jǐ gè **nǚshēng**

我们班有几个女生？

yī èr sān sì wǔ liù

一、二、三、四、五、六。

xiànzài nǐmen lái cāi yī cāi zhègè **bǐnggān**
    guàn lǐbian yǒu jǐ kuài bǐnggān

现在、你们来猜一猜这个饼干罐里边有几
    块饼干？

shí shí-èr jiǔ shí-sān

十！十二！九！十三！

wǒmen dǎkāi lái kànkàn ba āiyā zāo le shì
    kōng de

我们打开来看看吧 . . . 哎呀、糟了！是空
    的！

shì shéi bǎ **bǐnggān** chī guāng le

是谁把饼干吃光了？

Lluó Bīn nǐ shǒu shàng yǒu shénme

罗斌 . . . 你手上有什么？

Good morning, class! Today we are going to
    count **numbers**.

How many **girls** are in the class?

One, *two*, *three*, *four*, *five*, and *six*.

Now, how many cookies do you think there are in
    the **cookie jar**?

Ten! Twelve! Nine! Thirteen!

Let's see . . . Oh, no! It is empty!

Who ate the **cookies**?

Robin . . . what's that in your hands?

yī
一

èr
二

sān
三

sì
四

wǒ ài wǒde chǒngwù
我爱我的宠物　　I Love My Pets

wǒ yào yǎng yī zhī xiǎo māomī
我要养一只小猫咪

I Want a Kitty

*māma wǒde péngyou **Lìshā** xīn yǎng le yī zhī xīn de xiǎo māomī*
妈妈、我的朋友丽莎新养了一只新的小猫咪。

*Mommy, my friend **Lisa** has a new kitty.*

wǒ yě xiǎng yào
我也想要！

I want one too!

dànshì wǒmen zhèlǐ yǐjīng shì yī gè xiǎo dòngwùyuán le
但是我们这里已经是一个小动物园了。

But we already have a small zoo here.

wǒmen lái kànkàn yī zhī **gǒu** sì zhī **qīngwā**
我们来看看：一只狗、四只青蛙、

Let's see: one **dog**, four **frogs**,

sān zhī **cāngshǔ** yī zhī **wūguī** háiyǒu yī zhī **xīyì**
三只仓鼠、一只乌龟、还有一只蜥蜴！

three **hamsters**, one **turtle**, and one **lizard**!

*kěshì xiǎo māomī hǎo **kěài***
可是小猫咪好可爱. . .

*But little kittens are so **cute** . . .*

māo shuì zài nǎli ne
猫睡在哪里呢？

And where is the **cat** going to sleep?

*shuì zài wǒde **chuáng** shàng*
睡在我的床上。

*In my **bed**.*

shéi qù qīnglǐ xiāngzi lǐ de māo **fènbiàn** hé **niàoniào** ne
谁去清理箱子里的猫粪便和尿尿呢？

And who is going to clean the box with the **poop** and **pee**?

māma nàxiē dōngxi hěn hěn zāng wǒ bù xǐhuān
妈妈、那些东西很很脏。我不喜欢。

Mommy, that's yucky. I don't like that.

cāngshǔ
仓鼠

wūguī
乌龟

xīyì
蜥蜴

māo
猫

dài xiǎogǒu qù shàngxué
带小狗去上学

My Dog Goes to Dog School

hāi wǒ shì **xùn gǒu shī** 嗨！我是驯狗师。	Hi! I'm the **dog trainer**.
nǐde gǒu jiào shénme **míngzi** 你的狗叫什么名字？	What's your dog's **name**?
Mǎkè 马克。	*Mark.*
hāi Mǎkè wǒmen lái kànkàn nǐ huì zuò xiē shénme 嗨、马克。我们来看看你会做些什么。	Hi, Mark. Let's see what you can do.
mǎkè **zuò xià** 马克、坐下！	Mark, **sit**!
xiànzài Mǎkè **gēn wǒ** zǒu 现在、马克、跟我走！	Now, Mark, walk **with me**!
Mǎkè xiànzài qù jiē zhè gè **bàngzi** 马克、现在去接这个棒子！	Now, Mark, go fetch this **stick**!
hǎo a tā jiē zhù le guāi háizi Mǎkè 好啊！他接住了！乖孩子、马克！	*Yeah! He got it! Good boy, Mark!*
*Mǎkè **kuài** pǎo pǎo a pǎo a pǎo a* 马克、快跑！跑啊、跑啊、跑啊！	*Mark, run **fast**! Go, go, go!*

gǒu
狗

fènbiàn
粪便

zuò xià
坐下

pǎo
跑

wǒmen qù lǚyóu
我们去旅游
We're Going on a Trip

zài fēijīchǎng
在飞机场

At the Airport

qǐng bǎ **hùzhào** ná chūlái
请把护照拿出来。

Passports, please.

nǐmen jīntiān qù shénme dìfāng **lǚyóu**
你们今天去什么地方旅游？

Where are you **traveling** today?

qù **Zhōngguó** Běijing
去中国北京。

To Beijing, **China**.

xièxiè zhè shì nǐmende hùzhào hé **xíngli** tuōyùn dān
谢谢。这是你们的护照和行李托运单。

Thank you. Here are your passports, and these tickets are for the **suitcases**.

wǒmen qù nǎli
我们去哪里？

Where are we going?

wǒmen qù **dēng jī mén** zài nàli wǒmen shàng **fēijī**
我们去登机门。在那里我们上飞机。

To the **boarding gate**. That's the door to board the **airplane**.

wǒ yào shàng cèsuǒ
我要上厕所。

I want to go to the bathroom.

děng yī děng ràng wǒmen xiān zhǎodào zuòwèi zài qù
等一等、让我们先找到座位再去。

Wait, we need to find our seats first.

sānshí èr **pái** zhè jiù shì wǒmende **zuòwèi**
三十二排。这就是我们的座位！

Row thirty-two. Here are our **seats**!

Did You Know?

The Great Wall of China (5,500 miles from eastern to western China) was built more than two thousand years ago by the first Emperor of China (Qin Shi Huang) to provide a defense against northern invaders. In Chinese, the wall is called wànlǐ chángchéng 万里长城, which means the ten thousand li long wall. A "li" is a Chinese unit of measurement for length. Two li are equal to one kilometer.

hùzhào
护照

cèsuǒ
厕所

zuòwèi
座位

xíngli
行李

zài lǚguǎn
在旅馆

At the Hotel

wǒmen **jǐn wǎn** shuì zài zhèlǐ ma
我们今晚睡在这里吗？

*Are we going to sleep here **tonight**?*

shì de wǒmen míngtiān yī dà **zǎo** yào
    qǐchuáng suǒyǐ qù shuìjiào ba
是的、我们明天一大早要起床、所以去睡
    觉吧。

Yes, and tomorrow we'll leave **early**, so go to bed

wǒ bú **lèi**
我不累。

*I'm not **tired**.*

shì shì qù shuì yīxià **wǎnān**
试试去睡一下。晚安！

Try to sleep. **Good night!**

qǐchuáng lā wǒmen yào qù zuò **lǚyóu bāshì**
起床啦！我们要去坐旅游巴士。

Wake up! We have to take the **tour bus**.

qǐng bǎ **piào** ná chūlái xièxiè
请把票拿出来！谢谢。

Tickets, please! Thank you.

wǒmen dào le méiyǒu
我们到了没有？

Are we there yet?

bié zài wèn le jiù kuài dào le
别再问了。就快到了。

Stop asking. We are almost there.

kuài kàn nǐ kàndào **shān** shàng de
    Chángchéng ma
快看！你看到山上的长城吗？

Look! Can you see the **Great Wall** up on the
    mountain?

*wa zhēn **cháng** yā*
哇！真长呀！

*Wow! It's so **long**!*

bāshì
巴士

lǚguǎn
旅馆

shān
山

Chángchéng
长城

About the Authors

Ana Lomba's breakthrough method "Ana Lomba's Easy Immersion®" is changing the way people think about and interact with young children learning languages. Ana's lively resources and detailed lesson plans are favorites with teachers and parents who want to nurture young children's innate language abilities. A Princeton University graduate, Ana has taught Spanish from preschool to college and held leadership positions with national language organizations in the United States. Ana is a native of Madrid, Spain, and she lives with her husband and three children in Princeton, New Jersey. For more information about Ana's teaching resources, e-storybook collections, and iPad applications, go to www.analomba.com.

Marcela Summerville is the founder of Spanish Workshop for Children, an

Frank D. Jacobs

award-winning Spanish immersion program for young children in Philadelphia. Marcela is also a workshop presenter sharing her innovative teaching methodology at prestigious conferences across North America. In addition, she has published articles on teaching a second language to youth. Marcela is a native of Patagonia, Argentina, and she lives with her husband and two children in Philadelphia. For more information, visit www.spanishworkshopforchildren.com.

Lucy Chu Lee 竹露茜 has taught Chinese at Livingston High School in New Jersey for more than twenty years and is a teacher educator at Rutgers, The State University of New Jersey, and William Paterson University. She also coauthored the CLASS Professional Standards for K-12 Chinese Language Teachers. A native of China, she currently lives in Livingston, New Jersey, with her mother, two children, and two grandchildren.

Pedro Pérez del Solar, a native of Peru, holds a Ph.D. in Spanish Literature from Princeton University and has been a press illustrator since 1990. Pedro is currently an assistant professor of Spanish Literature and Culture at the University of Texas at El Paso.